Edward Thurston Hiscox

The star book on Baptist church polity

Edward Thurston Hiscox

The star book on Baptist church polity

ISBN/EAN: 9783337043216

Printed in Europe, USA, Canada, Australia, Japan

Cover: Foto ©ninafisch / pixelio.de

More available books at **www.hansebooks.com**

THE STAR BOOK

ON

BAPTIST CHURCH POLITY.

BY

REV. E. T. HISCOX, D. D.

Author of Baptist Church Directory, Baptist Short Method, Star Book Series, etc.

New York:

WARD & DRUMMOND,

Successors to U. D. WARD,

116 Nassau Street.

THE

STAR BOOK

ON

BAPTIST CHURCH POLITY,

BY

REV. E. T. HISCOX, D.D.

AUTHOR OF BAPTIST CHURCH DIRECTORY, BAPTIST SHORT METHOD, STAR BOOK SERIES, &C., &C.

EIGHTEENTH THOUSAND.

NEW YORK:

WARD & DRUMMOND,

Successors to U. D. WARD,

NO. 116 NASSAU STREET.

Entered, according to Act of Congress, in the year 1880, by

WARD & DRUMMOND,

Successors to U. D. Ward,

In the office of the Librarian of Congress, at Washington, D. C.

PREFACE

TO THE REVISED AND ENLARGED EDITION.

It is probably safe to say, that two-thirds of the cases of strife and division which rend the churches and scandalize religion, are due to misjudged and misdirected proceedings in Church business, and in the exercise of discipline. It is of the utmost importance, that, not only pastors and deacons, but the members generally, should understand what constitutes correct action, since on their vote depend decisions which involve the most serious consequences to the churches.

Many of the churches have prepared for themselves brief manuals, embracing articles of faith, covenant, rules of order, with various statements of principles. But the greater part of them are very imperfect, and not a few are very erroneous, and misguiding in some of their positions and principles.

The object of this little work is to provide a brief manual, which will serve as a guide in the more important concerns, as well as in the ordinary experience of the churches. Its statements and principles, so far as they go, are sanctioned by the almost universal usages of our churches, and will generally be accepted and approved by the best authorities, on the most careful examination. It is in strict accordance with the larger work, the Baptist Church Directory, prepared by the author, and published many years ago, great numbers of which have been circulated in all sections of the country, and which is generally accepted as a standard in matters of Baptist Church polity; and which has passed into five or six translations, and is in general use on our foreign mission fields.

The present edition is much improved by a careful revision, and also by the addition of considerable new matter. The Scripture references to the Articles of Faith, omitted in the first editions to save space and expense, have in this been supplied, while, at the same time, the price has been reduced.

The need of such a manual, and the value of this to supply the want, are certified by the large sale it has already had, and the universal commendation it has received.

It is hoped the pastors and their churches will see the advantage of putting a copy of the Star Book into the hands of every member, and of every candidate for admission.

Its general adoption could not fail to add much to the uniformity of Church action, and the harmony of Church life.

E. T. H.

NEW YORK, *March* 10, 1880.

ARTICLES OF FAITH.

I.—THE SCRIPTURES.

We believe that the Holy Bible was written by men divinely inspired, and is a perfect treasure of heavenly instruction;[1] that it has God for its author, salvation for its end,[2] and truth without any mixture of error for its matter;[3] that it reveals the principles by which God will judge us;[4] and therefore is, and shall remain to the end of the world, the true centre of Christian union,[5] and the supreme standard by which all human conduct, creeds, and opinions should be tried.[6]

---

[1] 2 Tim. iii. 16, 17. All Scripture is given by inspiration of God, and is profitable for doctrine, for reproof, for correction, for instruction in righteousness; that the man of God may be perfect, thoroughly furnished unto all good works. Also, 2 Pet. i. 21. 2 Sam. xxiii. 2. Acts i. 16; iii. 21. John x. 35. Luke xvi. 29–31. Ps. cxix. 111. Rom. iii. 1, 2.

[2] 2 Tim. iii. 15. Able to make thee wise unto salvation. Also, 1 Pet. i. 10–12. Acts xi. 14. Rom. i. 16. Mark xvi. 16. John v. 38–39.

[3] Proverbs xxx. 5, 6. Every word of God is pure. Add thou not unto his words, lest he reprove thee, and thou be found a liar. Also, John xvii. 17. Rev. xxii. 18, 19. Rom. iii. 4.

[4] Rom. ii. 12. As many as have sinned in the law, shall be judged by the law. John xii. 47, 48. If any man hear my words—the word that I have spoken, the same shall judge him in the last day. Also, 1 Cor. iv. 3, 4. Luke x. 10–16; xii. 47, 48.

[5] Phil. iii. 16. Let us walk by the same rule; let us mind the same thing. Also, Ephes. iv. 3, 6. Phil. ii. 1, 2. 1 Cor. i. 10. 1 Pet. iv. 11.

[6] 1 John iv. 1. Beloved, believe not every spirit, but try the spirits whether they are of God. Isaiah viii. 20. To the law and to the testimony; If they speak not according to this word, it is because there is no light in them. 1 Thess. v. 21. 2 Cor. xiii. 5. Acts xvii. 11. 1 John iv. 6. Jude 3. 5. Ephes. vi. 17. Ps. cxix. 59, 60. Phil. i. 9–11.

II.—The True God.

We believe the Scriptures teach that there is one, and only one, living and true God, an infinite, intelligent Spirit, whose name is JEHOVAH, the Maker and Supreme Ruler of Heaven and Earth:[1] inexpressibly glorious in holiness,[2] and worthy of all possible honor, confidence and love;[3] that in the unity of the Godhead there are three persons, the Father, the Son, and the Holy Ghost;[4] equal in every divine perfection, and executing distinct but harmonious offices in the great work of redemption.[6]

[1] John iv. 24. God is a Spirit. Ps. cxlvii. 5. His understanding is infinite. Ps. lxxxiii. 18. Thou whose name alone is JEHOVAH, art the Most High over all the earth. Heb. iii. 4. Rom. i. 20. Jer. x. 10.

[2] Ex. xv. 11. Who is like unto Thee—glorious in holiness? Isa. vi. 3. 1 Pet. i. 15, 16. Rev. iv. 6–8.

[3] Mark xii. 30. Thou shalt love the Lord thy God with all thy heart, and with all thy soul, and with all thy mind, and with all thy strength. Rev. iv. 11. Thou art worthy, O Lord, to receive glory, and honor, and power. Matt. x. 37. Jer. ii. 12, 13.

[4] Matt. xxviii. 19. Go ye therefore and teach all nations, baptizing them in the name of the Father, and of the Son, and of the Holy Ghost. John xv. 26. 1 Cor. xii. 4–6. 1 John v. 7.

[5] John x. 30. I and my Father are one. John v. 17; xiv. 23; xvii. 5, 10. Acts v. 3, 4. 1 Cor. ii. 10, 11. Phil. ii. 5, 6.

[6] Ephes. ii. 18. For through Him [the Son] we both have an access by one Spirit unto the Father. 2 Cor. xiii. 14. The grace of our Lord Jesus Christ, and the love of God, and the communion of the Holy Ghost, be with you all. Rev. i. 4,5.

III.—The Fall of Man.

We believe the Scriptures teach that Man was created in holiness, under the law of his Maker; but by voluntary transgression fell from that holy and happy state;[2] in consequence of which all mankind are now sinners,[3] not by constraint but choice;[4] being by nature utterly void of that holiness required by the law of God, positively inclined to evil; and therefore under just condemnation to eternal ruin,[5] without defense or excuse.[6]

---

[1] Gen. i. 27. God created man in his own image. Gen. i. 31. And God saw everything that he had made, and behold, it was very good. Eccles. vii. 29. Acts. xvii. 26. Gen. ii. 16.

[2] Gen. iii. 6-24. And when the woman saw that the tree was good for food, and that it was pleasant to the eyes, and a tree to be desired to make one wise; she took of the fruit thereof, and did eat; and gave also unto her husband with her, and he did eat. Rom. v. 12.

[3] Rom. v. 19. By one man's disobedience many were made sinners. John iii. 6. Ps. li. 5. Rom. v. 15-19; viii. 7.

[4] Isa. liii. 6. We have turned, every one to his own way. Gen. vi. 12. Rom. iii. 9-18.

[5] Eph. ii. 3. Among whom also we all had our conversation in times past in the lusts of our flesh, fulfilling the desires of the flesh and of the mind; and were by nature the children of wrath even as others. Rom. i. 18. Rom. i. 32; ii. 1-16. Gal. iii. 10. Matt. xx. 15.

[6] Ez. xviii. 19, 20. The soul that sinneth it shall die. The son shall not bear the iniquity of the father, neither shall the father bear the iniquity of the son. Rom. i. 20. So that they are without excuse. Rom. iii. 19. That every mouth may be stopped and all the world may become guilty before God. Gal. iii. 22.

IV.—The Way of Salvation.

We believe the Scriptures teach that the salvation of sinners is wholly of grace; [1] through the mediatorial offices of the Son of God; [2] who by the appointment of the Father, freely took upon him our nature, yet without sin; [3] honored the divine law by his personal obedience, [4] and by his death made a full atonement for our sins; [5] that having risen from the dead, he is now enthroned in heaven; [6] and uniting in his wonderful person the tenderest sympathies with divine perfections, he is every way qualified to be a suitable, a compasssionate and an all-sufficient Saviour. [7]

---

[1] Eph. ii. 5. By grace ye are saved. Matt. xviii. 11. 1 John iv. 10. 1 Cor. iii. 5-7. Acts xv. 11.

[2] John iii. 16. For God so loved the world that he gave his only begotten Son, that whosoever believeth in him should not perish, but have everlasting life. John i. 1-14. Heb. iv. 14; xii. 24.

[3] Phil. ii. 6, 7. Who being in the form of God, thought it not robbery to be equal with God; but made himself of no reputation, and took upon him the form of a servant, and was made in the likeness of men. Heb. ii. 9; ii. 14. 2 Cor. v. 21.

[4] Isa. xlii. 21. The Lord is well pleased for his righteousness' sake: he will magnify the law and make it honorable. Phil. ii. 8. Gal. iv. 4, 5. Rom. iii. 21.

[5] Isa. liii. 4, 5. He was wounded for our transgressions, he was bruised for our iniquities; the chastisement of our peace was upon him; and with his stripes we are healed. Matt. xx. 28. Rom. iii. 21; iv. 25-26. 1 John iv. 10; ii. 2. 1 Cor. xv. 1-3. Heb. ix. 13-15.

[6] 1 Peter iii. 22. Who is gone into Heaven, and is on the right hand of God, angels and authorities and powers being made subject unto Him. Heb. ix. 24. Heb. i. 3; viii. 1. Col. iii. 1-4.

[7] Heb. vii. 25. Wherefore he is able also to save them to the uttermost that come unto God by him, seeing he ever liveth to make intercession for them. Col. ii. 9. For in him dwelleth all the fulness of the Godhead bodily. Heb. ii. 18. Heb. vii. 26. Ps. lxxxix. 19. Ps. xlv.

V.—JUSTIFICATION.

We believe the Scriptures teach that the great Gospel blessing which Christ [1] secures to such as believe in Him is justification; [2] that justification includes the pardon of sin, [3] and the promise of eternal life on principles of righteousness; [4] that it is bestowed, not in consideration of any works of righteousness which we have done, but solely through faith in the Redeemer's blood; [5] by virtue of which faith his perfect righteousness is freely imputed to us of God; [6] that it brings us into a state of most blessed peace and favor with God, and secures every other blessing needful for time and eternity. [7]

[1] John i. 16. Of his fullness have all we received. Eph. iii. 8.

[2] Acts xiii. 39. By him all that believe are justified from all things. Isa. iii. 11, 12. Rom. v.ii. 1.

[3] Rom. v. 9. Being justified by his blood, we shall be saved from wrath through him. Zech. xiii. 1. Matt. ix. 6. Acts x. 43.

[4] Rom. v. 17. They which receive the abundance of grace and of the gift of righteousness, shall reign in life by one, Jesus Christ. Titus iii. 5, 6. 1 Pet. iii. 7. 1 John ii. 25. Rom. v. 21.

[5] Rom. iv. 4, 5. Now to him that worketh is the reward not reckoned of grace, but of debt. But to him that worketh not, but believeth on him that justifieth the ungodly his faith is counted for righteousness. Rom. v. 21; vi. 23. Phil. iii. 7-9.

[6] Rom. v. 19. By the obedience of one shall many be made righteous. Rom. iii. 24-26; iv. 23-25. 1 John ii. 12.

[7] Rom. v. 1, 2. Being justified by faith, we have peace with God, through our Lord Jesus Christ; by whom also we have access by faith into this grace wherein we stand, and rejoice in hope of the glory of God. Rom. v. 3. Rom. v. 11. 1 Cor. i. 30, 31. Mat. vi. 33. 1 Tim. iv. 8.

VI.—The Freeness of Salvation.

We believe the Scriptures teach that the blessings of salvation are made free to all by the Gospel:[1] that it is the immediate duty of all to accept them by a cordial, penitent and obedient faith;[2] and that nothing prevents the salvation of the greatest sinner on earth, but his own determined depravity and voluntary rejection of the Gospel;[3] which rejection involves him in an aggravated condemnation.[4]

[1] Isa. lv. 1. Ho, every one that thirsteth, come ye to the waters. Rev. xxii. 17. Whosoever will let him take the water of life freely. Luke xiv. 17.

[2] Acts xvii. 30. And the times of this ignorance God winked at, but now commandeth all men everywhere to repent. Rom. xvi. 26. Mark i. 15. Rom. i. 15-17.

[3] John v. 40. Ye will not come to me, that ye might have life. Matt. xxiii. 37. Rom. ix. 32. Prov. i. 24. Acts xiii. 46.

[4] John iii. 19. And this is the condemnation, that light is come into the world, and men loved darkness rather than light because their deeds were evil. Matt. xi. 20. Luke xix. 27. 2 Thess. i. 8.

VII.—Regeneration.

We believe the Scriptures teach that in order to be saved, sinners must be regenerated, or born again;[1] that regeneration consists in giving a holy disposition to the mind;[2] that it is effected in a manner above our comprehension by the power of the Holy Spirit, in connection with divine truth,[3] so as to secure our voluntary obedience to the Gospel;[4] and that its proper evidence appears in the holy fruits of repentance, and faith and newness of life.[5]

---

[1] John iii. 3. Verily, verily, I say unto thee, except a man be born again, he cannot see the kingdom of God. John iii. 6, 7. 1 Cor. i. 14. Rev. viii. 7-9; Rev. xxi. 27.

[2] 2 Cor. v. 17. If any man be in Christ, he is a new creature. Ez. xxxvi. 26. Deut. xxx. 6. Rom. ii. 28, 29; v. 5. 1 John, iv. 7.

[3] John iii. 8. The wind bloweth where it listeth, and thou hearest the sound thereof, but canst not tell whence it cometh, and whither it goeth; so is every one that is born of the Spirit. John i. 13. James i. 16–18. 1 Cor. i. 30. Phil. ii. 13.

[4] 1 Pet. i. 22–25. Ye have purified your souls in obeying the truth through the Spirit. 1 John v. 1. Eph. iv. 20–24; Col. iii. 9–11.

[5] Eph. v. 9. The fruit of the Spirit is in all goodness and righteousness, and truth. Rom. viii. 9. Gal. v. 16–23. Eph. iii. 14–21. Matt. iii. 8–10; vii. 20. 1 John v. 4, 18.

VIII.—Repentance and Faith.

We believe the Scriptures teach that repentance and faith are sacred duties, and also inseparable graces, wrought in our souls by the regenerating Spirit of God;[1] whereby being deeply convinced of our guilt, danger and helplessness, and of the way of salvation by Christ,[2] we turn to God with unfeigned contrition, confession, and supplication for mercy;[3] at the same time heartily receiving the Lord Jesus Christ as our prophet, priest, and king, and relying on him alone as the only and all-sufficient Saviour.[4]

---

[1] Mark i. 15. Repent ye, and believe the Gospel. Acts xi. 18. Then hath God also to the Gentiles granted repentance unto life. Ephes. ii. 8. By grace ye are saved, through faith; and that not of yourselves; it is the gift of God. 1 John v. 1.

[2] John xvi. 8. He will reprove the world of sin, and of righteousness, and of judgment. Acts II. 38. Then Peter said unto them, Repent, and be baptized every one of you in the name of Jesus Christ for the remission of sins. Acts xvi. 30, 31.

[3] Luke xviii. 13. And the publican smote upon his breast, saying, God be merciful to me a sinner. Luke xv. 18–21. James iv. 7–10. 2 Cor. vii. 11. Rome x. 12, 13 Ps. li.

[4] Rom. x. 9–11. If thou shalt confess with thy mouth the Lord Jesus, and shalt believe in thy heart that God hath raised him from the dead, thou shalt be saved. Acts iii. 22, 23. Heb. iv. 14. Ps. ii. 6. Heb. i. 8; viii. 25. 2 Tim. i. 12.

IX.—God's Purpose of Grace.

We believe the Scriptures teach that election is the eternal purpose of God, according to which he graciously regenerates, sanctifies and saves sinners;[1] that being perfectly consistent with the free agency of man, it comprehends all the means in connection with the end;[2] that it is a most glorious display of God's sovereign goodness, being infinitely free, wise, holy and unchangeable;[3] that it utterly excludes boasting, and promotes humility, love, prayer, praise, trust in God, and active imitation of his free mercy;[4] that it encourages the use of means in the highest degree; that it may be ascertained by its effects in all who truly believe the Gospel;[6] that it is the foundation of Christian assurance;[7] and that to ascertain it with regard to ourselves demands and deserves the utmost diligence.[8]

---

[1] 2 Tim. i. 8, 9. But be thou partaker of the afflictions of the Gospel, according to the power of God; who hath saved us and called us with a holy calling, not according to our works, but according to his own purpose and grace which was given us in Christ Jesus before the world began. Eph. i. 3–14. 1 Pet. i. 1, 2. Rom. xi. 5, 6. John xv. 16. 1 John iv. 19. Hos. xii. 9.

[2] 2 Thess. ii. 13, 14. But we are bound to give thanks always to God for you, brethren beloved of the Lord, because God hath from the beginning chosen you to salvation, through sanctification of the Spirit and belief of the truth; whereunto he called you by our Gospel, to the obtaining of the glory of our Lord Jesus Christ. Acts xiii. 48. John x. 16. Matt. xx. 16. Acts xv. 14.

[3] Ex. xxxiii. 18, 19. And he said, I will cause all my goodness to pass before thee, and I will proclaim the name of the Lord before thee, and will be gracious to whom I will be gracious, and will show mercy on whom I will show mercy. Matt. xx. 15. Eph. i. 11. Rom. ix. 23, 24. Jer. xxxi. 3. Rom. xi. 28, 29. Jam. i. 17, 18. 2 Tim. i. 9. Rom. xi. 32–36.

[4] 1 Cor. iv. 7. For who maketh thee to differ from another? and what hast thou that thou didst not receive? Now if thou didst receive it, why dost thou glory as if thou hadst not received it? 1 Cor. i. 26–31. Rom. iii. 27; iv. 16. Col. iii. 12. 1 Cor. iii. 5–7; xv. 10.

[5] 2 Tim. ii. 10. Therefore I endure all things for the elects' sake, that they also may obtain the salvation which is in Christ Jesus with eternal glory. 1 Cor. ix. 22. Rom. viii. 28–30. John vi. 37–40. 2 Pet. i. 10.

[6] 1 Thess. 4, 10. Knowing, brethren beloved, your election of God.

[7] Rom. viii. 28–30. Moreover, whom he did predestinate, them he also called, and whom he called them he also justified, and whom he justified them he also glorified. Isa. xlii. 16. Rom. xi. 29.

[8] 2 Pet. i. 10, 11. Wherefore the rather, brethren, give diligence to make your calling and election sure. Phil. iii. 12. Heb. vi. 11.

X. Santification.

We believe the Scriptures teach that Sanctification is the process by which, according to the will of God, we are made partakers of his holiness;[1] that it is a progressive work;[2] that it is begun in regeneration;[3] that it is carried on in the hearts of believers by the presence and power of the Holy Spirit, the Sealer and Comforter, in the continual use of the appointed means—especially the word of God--self-examination, self-denial, watchfulness, and prayer;[4] and in the practice of all godly exercises and duties.[5]

---

[1] Thess. iv. 3. For this is the will of God, even your santification. 1. Thess. v. 23. And the very God of peace sanctify you wholly. 2 Cor. vii. 1; xiii. 9. Ephes. i. 4.

[2] Prov. iv. 18. The path of the just is as the shining light, which shineth more and more, unto the perfect day. 2 Cor. iii. 18. Heb. vi. 1. 2 Peter i. 5–8. Phil. 12–16.

[3] 1 John ii. 29. If ye know that He-[God], is righteous, ye know that every one that doeth righteousness is born of Him. Rom. viii. 5. John iii. 6. Phil. i. 9–11. Ephes. i. 13, 14.

[4] Phil. ii. 12, 13. Work out your own salvation with fear and trembling, for it is God which worketh in you both to will and to do, of his good pleasure. Ephes. iv. 11, 12. 1 Peter ii. 2. 2 Peter iii. 18. 2 Cor. xiii. 5. Luke xi. 35; ix. 23. Matt. xxvi. 41. Ephes. vi. 18; iv. 30.

[5] 1 Tim. 4, 7. Exercise thyself unto godliness.

XI.—Perseverance of Saints.

We believe the Scriptures teach that such only are real believers as endure unto the end:[1] that their persevering attachment to Christ is the grand mark which distinguishes them from superficial professors;[2] that a special Providence watches over their welfare;[3] and they are kept by the power of God through faith unto salvation.[4]

---

[1] John viii. 31. Then said Jesus, If ye continue in my word, then are ye my disciples indeed. 1 John ii. 27, 28; iii. 9; v. 18.

John ii. 19. They went out from us, but they were not of us; for if they had been of us, they would no doubt have continued with us; but they went out that it might be made manifest that they were not all of us. John xiii. 18. Matt. xiii. 20, 21. John vi. 66–69.

[3] Rom. viii. 28. And we know all things work together for good unto them that love God, to them who are the called according to his purpose. Matt. vi. 30–33. Jer. xxxii. 40. Ps. xci. 11, 12; cxxi. 3.

[4] Phil. i. 6. He who hath begun a good work in you will perform it until the day of Jesus Christ. Phil. ii. 12, 13. Jude 24. 25. Heb. i. 14; xiii. 5. 2 Kings vi, 16. 1 John iv. 4.

XII.—THE LAW AND GOSPEL.

We believe the Scriptures teach that the Law of God is the eternal and unchangeable rule of his moral government;[1] that it is holy, just, and good;[2] and that the inability which the Scriptures ascribe to fallen men to fulfill its precepts arises entirely from their sinful nature;[3] to deliver them from which, and to restore them through a Mediator to unfeigned obedience to the holy Law, is one great end of the Gospel, and of the Means of Grace connected with the establishment of the visible church.[4]

---

[1] Rom. iii. 31. Do we make void the law through faith? God forbid. Yea, we establish the law. Matt. v. 17. Luke, xvi. 17. Rom. iii. 20; iv. 15.

[2] Rom. vii. 12. The Law is holy, and the commandment holy, and just, and good. Rom. vii. 7, 14, 22. Gal. iii. 21. Psalm cxix.

[3] Rom. viii. 7, 8. The carnal mind is enmity against God; for it is not subject to the law of God, neither indeed can be. So then they that are in the flesh cannot please God. Josh. xxiv. 19. Jer. xiii. 23. John vi. 44; v. 44.

[4] Rom. viii. 2, 4. For the law of the Spirit of Life in Christ Jesus hath made me free from the law of sin and death. For what the law could not do, in that it was weak through the flesh, God sending his own Son in the likeness of sinful flesh, and for sin, condemned sin in the flesh; that the righteousness of the law might be fulfilled in us, who walk not after the flesh, but after the Spirit. Rom. x. 4. 1 Tim. i. 5. Heb. viii. 10. Jude, 20, 21. Heb. xii. 14. Matt. xvi. 17, 18. 1 Cor. xii. 28.

XIII.—A Gospel Church.

We believe the Scriptures teach that a visible Church of Christ is a congregation of baptized believers,[1] associated by covenant in the faith and fellowship of the Gospel; [2] observing the ordinances of Christ; [3] governed by his laws; [4] and exercising the gifts, rights, and privileges invested in them by His word; [5] that its only scriptural officers are Bishops or Pastors, and Deacons,[6] whose qualifications, claims, and duties are defined in the Epistles to Timothy and Titus.

---

1 Acts ii. 41, 42. Then they that gladly received his word were baptized; and the same day there were added to them about three thousand souls. Acts v. 11; viii. 1; xi. 31; 1 Cor. iv. 17; 1 Tim. iii. 5.

2 2 Cor. viii. 5. They first gave their own selves to the Lord, and unto us by the will of God. Acts ii. 47. 1 Cor. v. 11, 18.

3 1 Cor. xi. 2. Now I praise you, brethren, that ye remember me in all things, and keep the ordinances as I delivered them to you. 2 Thess. iii. 7. Rom. xvi. 17-20. 1 Cor. xi. 23. Matt. xviii. 15-20. 1 Cor. v. 5.

4 Matt. xxviii. 20. Teaching them to observe all things whatsoever I have commanded you. John xiv. 15; xv. 1 John iv. 21. 1 Thes. iv. 2. 2 John 6.

5 Ephes. iv. 7. Unto every one of us is given grace according to the measure of the gift of Christ. 1 Cor. xiv. 12. Seek that ye may excel to the edifying of the church.

Phil. i. 1. With the Bishops and Deacons. Acts xiv. 23; xv. 22. I Tim. iii. Titus i.

XIV.—CHRISTIAN BAPTISM.

We believe the Scriptures teach that Christian Baptism is the immersion in water of a believer in Christ, [1] into the name of the Father, and Son, and Holy Ghost; [2] to show forth in a solemn and beautiful emblem, our faith in the crucified, buried, and risen Saviour, with its effect, in our death to sin and resurrection to a new life; [3] that it is prerequisite to the privileges of a church relation, and to the Lord's Supper.[4]

---

[1] Acts viii. 36-39. And the eunuch said, See, here is water; what doth hinder me to be baptized? And Philip said, If thou believest with all thy heart thou mayest. . . . And they went down into the water, both Philip and the eunuch, and he baptized him. Matt. iii. 5, 6. John iii. 22, 23; iv. 1, 2. Matt. xxviii. 19. Mark xvi. 16. Acts ii. 38; viii. 12; xvi. 32-34; xviii. 8.

[2] Matt. xviii. 19. Baptizing them in the name of the Father, and of the Son, and of the Holy Ghost. Acts x. 47, 48. Gal. iii. 27, 28.

[3] Rom. vi. 4. Therefore we are buried with him by baptism into death; that like as Christ was raised from the dead by the glory of the Father, even so we also, should walk in newness of life. Col. ii. 12. 1 Peter iii. 20, 21. Acts xxii. 16.

[4] Acts, ii. 41, 42. Then they that gladly received his word were baptized, and there were added to them, the same day, about three thousand souls. And they continued steadfastly in the apostles' doctrine and fellowship, and in rebaking of bread, and in prayers. Matt. xxviii. 19, 20.

XV.—The Lord's Supper.

We believe the Scriptures teach that the Lord's Supper is a provision of bread and wine, as symbols of Christ's body and blood, partaken of by the members of the Church;[1] in commemoration of the suffering and death of their Lord;[2] showing their faith and participation in the merits of his sacrifice, and their hope of eternal life through his resurrection from the dead; its observance to be preceded by faithful self-examination.[3]

---

[1] Luke xxii. 19, 20. And he took bread, and gave thanks, and brake, and gave unto them, saying: This is my body which is given for you; this do in remembrance of me. Likewise also the cup after supper, saying, this cup is the New Testament in my blood, which is shed for you. Mark xiv. 20-26. Matt. xxvi. 27-30. 1 Cor. xi. 27–30. 1 Cor. x. 16.

[2] 1. Cor. xi. 26. For, as often as ye eat this bread, and drink this cup, ye do show the Lord's death until he come. Matt. xxviii. 20.

[3] 1 Cor. xi. 28. But let a man examine himself, and so let him eat of that bread, and drink of that cup. Acts ii. 42. 46; xx. 7, 11.

XVI.—The Christian Sabbath.

We believe the Scriptures teach that the first day of the week is the Lord's Day, or Christian Sabbath;[1] and is to be kept sacred to religious purposes,[2] by abstaining from all secular labor except works of mercy and necessity,[3] by the devout observance of all the means of grace, both private[4] and public;[5] and by preparation for that rest that remaineth for the people of God.[6]

---

1 Acts xx. 7. On the first day of the week, when the disciples came together to break bread, Paul preached to them. Gen. ii. 3. Col. ii. 16, 17. Mark ii. 27. John xx. 19. 1 Cor. xvi. 1, 2.

Ex. xx. 8. Remember the Sabbath Day, to keep it holy. Rev. i. 10. I was in the Spirit on the Lord's Day. Ps. cxviii. 24.

3 Isa. lviii. 13, 14. If thou turn away thy foot from the Sabbath, from doing thy pleasure on my holy day; and call the Sabbath a delight, the holy of the Lord honorable; and shalt honor him, not doing thine own ways, nor finding thine own pleasure, nor speaking thine own words; then shall thou delight thyself in the Lord, and I will cause thee to ride upon the high places of the earth, and feed thee with the heritage of Jacob. Isa. lvi. 2–8.

4 Ps. cxviii. 15. The voice of rejoicing and salvation is in the tabernacles of the righteous.

5 Heb. x. 24, 25. Not forsaking the assembling of yourselves together, as the manner of some is. Acts xiii. 44. The next Sabbath Day came almost the whole city together to hear the word of God. Lev. xix. 30. Ex. xlvi. 3. Luke iv. 16. Acts xvii. 2, 3. Ps. xxvi. 8; lxxxvii. 3.

6 Heb. iv. 3–11. Let us labor therefore to enter into that rest.

XVII.—Civil Government.

We believe the Scriptures teach that civil government is of divine appointment, for the interest and good order of human society;[1] and that magistrates are to be prayed for, conscientiously honored and obeyed;[2] except only in things opposed to the will of our Lord Jesus Christ,[3] who is the only Lord of the conscience, and the Prince of the kings of the earth.[4]

---

[1] Rom. xiii. 1–7. The powers that be are ordained of God. For rulers are not a terror to good works, but to the evil. Deut. xvi. 18. 2 Sam. xxiii. 3. Ex. xviii. 23. Jer. xxx. 21.

[2] Matt. xxii. 21. Render therefore unto Cæsar the things that are Cæsar's, and unto God the things that are God's. Titus iii. 1. 1 Pet. ii. 13. 1 Tim. ii. 1–8.

[3] Acts v. 29. We ought to obey God rather than man— Matt. x. 28. Fear not them which kill the body, but are not able to kill the soul. Dan. iii. 15–18; vi. 7, 10. Acts iv. 18–20.

[4] Matt. xxiii. 10. Ye have one Master, even Christ. Rom. xiv. 4. Who art thou that judgest another man's servant? Rev. xix. 14. And he hath on his vesture and on his thigh a name written, King of Kings and Lord of Lords. Ps. lxxii. 11. Ps. ii. Rom. xiv. 9–13.

XVIII.—Righteous and Wicked.

We believe the Scriptures teach that there is a radical and essential difference between the righteous and the wicked ;[1] that such only as through faith are justified in the name of the Lord Jesus, and sanctified by the Spirit of our God, are truly righteous in his esteem ;[2] while all such as continue in impenitence and unbelief are in his sight wicked and under the curse ;[3] and this distinction holds among men both in and after death.[4]

---

[1] Mal. iii. 18. Ye shall discern between the righteous and the wicked ; between him that serveth God and him that serveth him not. Prov. xii. 26. Isa. v. 20. Gen. xviii. 23. Jer. xv. 19. Acts x. 34, 35. Rom. vi. 16.

Rom. i. 17. The just shall live by faith. Rom. vii. 6. We are delivered from the law, that being dead wherein we were held, that we should serve in newness of spirit, and not in the oldness of the letter. 1 John ii. 29. If ye know that he is righteous, ye know that every one that doeth righteousness is born of him. 1 John iii. 7. Rom. vi. 18, 22. 1 Cor. xi. 32. Prov. xi. 31. 1 Pet. iv. 17, 18.

[3] 1 John v. 19. And we know that we are of God, and the whole world lieth in wickedness. Gal. iii. 10. As many as are of the works of the law, are under the curse. John iii. 36. Isa. lvii. 21. Ps. x. 4. Isa. lv. 6, 7.

[4] Prov. xiv. 32. The wicked is driven away in his wickedness, but the righteous hath hope in his death. Luke xvi. 25. Thou in thy lifetime receivedst thy good things, and likewise Lazarus evil things ; but now he is comforted, and thou art tormented. John viii. 21–24. Prov. x. 24. Luke xii. 4, 5 ; xi. 23–26. John xii. 25, 26. Eccl. iii. 17. Matt. vii. 13, 14.

XIX.—THE WORLD TO COME.

We believe the Scriptures teach that the end of the world is approaching;[1] that at the Last Day, Christ will descend from heaven,[2] and raise the dead from the grave for final retribution;[3] that a solemn separation will then take place;[4] that the wicked will be adjudged to endless punishment, and the righteous to endless joy;[5] and that this judgment will fix forever the final state of men in heaven or hell, on principles of righteousness.

---

[1] Pet. iv. 7. But the end of all things is at hand; be ye therefore sober, and watch unto prayer. 1 Cor. vii. 29–31. Heb. i. 10–12. Matt. xxiv. 35. 1 John ii. 17. Matt xxviii. 20; xiii. 39, 40. 2 Pet. iii. 3–13.

[2] Acts i. 11. This same Jesus which is taken up from you into heaven, shall so come in like manner as ye have seen him go into heaven. Rev. i. 7. Heb. ix. 28. Acts iii. 21. 1 Thess. iv. 13–18; v. 1–11.

[3] Acts xxiv. 15. There shall be a resurrection of the dead, both of the just and unjust. 1 Cor. xv. 12–59. Luke xiv. 14. Dan. xii. 2. John v. 28, 29; vi. 40; xi. 25, 26. 2 Tim. i. 10. Acts x. 42.

[4] Matt. xiii. 49. The angels shall come forth, and sever the wicked from among the just. Matt. xiii. 37–43; xxiv. 30, 31; xxv. 31–33.

[5] Matt. xxv. 35–41. And these shall go away into everlasting punishment, but the righteous into life eternal. Rev. xxii. 11. He that is unjust let him be unjust still; and he which is filthy let him be filthy still; and he that is righteous let him he righteous still; and he that is holy let him be holy still. 1 Cor. vi. 9, 10. Mark ix. 43–48.

2 Pet. ii. 9. Jude 7. Phi. iii. 19. Rom. vi. 22. 2 Cor. v. 10, 11. John iv. 36. 2 Cor. iv. 18.

[6] Rom. iii. 5, 6. Is God unrighteous, who taketh vengeance? (I speak as a man.) God forbid; for how then shall God judge the world? 2 Thess. i. 6–12. Seeing it is a righteous thing with God to recompense tribulation to them who trouble you, and to you who are troubled, rest with us—when he shall come to be glorified in his saints, and to be admired in all them that believe. Heb. vi. 1, 2. 1 Cor. iv. 5. Acts xvii. 31. Rom. ii. 2–16. Rev. xx. 11, 12. 1 John ii. 28; iv. 17.

SEEING THEN THAT ALL THESE THINGS SHALL BE DISSOLVED, WHAT MANNER OF PERSONS OUGHT YE TO BE IN ALL HOLY CONVERSATION AND GODLINESS, LOOKING FOR AND HASTING UNTO THE COMING OF THE DAY OF GOD? 2 Peter iii. 11, 12.

COVENANT.

Having been, as we trust, brought by divine grace to embrace the Lord Jesus Christ, and to give ourselves wholly to him, we do now solemnly and joyfully covenant with each other, TO WALK TOGETHER IN HIM, WITH BROTHERLY LOVE, to his glory, as our common Lord. We do, therefore, in his strength, engage—

That we will exercise a Christian care and watchfulness over each other, and faithfully warn, exhort, and admonish each other as occasion may require:

That we will not forsake the assembling of ourselves together, but will uphold the public worship of God, and the ordinances of his house:

That we will not omit closet and family religion at home, nor neglect the great duty of religiously training our children, and those under our care, for the service of Christ, and the enjoyment of heaven:

That, as we are the light of the world, and salt of the earth, we will seek divine aid, to enable us to deny ungodliness, and every worldly lust, and to walk circumspectly in the world, that we may win the souls of men:

That we will cheerfully contribute of our property, according as God has prospered us, for the maintainance of a faithful and evangelical ministry among us, for the support of the poor, and to spread the Gospel over the earth:

That we will in all conditions, even till death, strive to live to the glory of him who hath called us out of darkness into his marvellous light.

"And may the God of peace, who brought again from the dead our Lord Jesus, that great Shepherd of the sheep, through the blood of the everlasting covenant, make us perfect in every good work, to do his will, working in us that which is well pleasing in his sight through Jesus Christ; to whom be glory, forever and ever. Amen."

A CHRISTIAN CHURCH.

A Christian Church is *a congregation of baptized believers in Christ* united in covenant, worshipping together, associated in the faith and fellowship of the gospel, practising its precepts, observing its ordinances, recognizing and receiving Christ as their supreme lawgiver and ruler, and taking His Word as their exclusive and sufficient rule of faith and practice, in all matters of religion.

That a Christian Church is a congregation of believers, and not a society or number of congregations or churches united under some more general head or government, is evident from the mention made of the apostolic churches in the New Testament. By such mention we learn that *churches* were single, separate, visible congregations of regenerated persons, organized with their laws, officers, ordinances, discipline and duties, doing the work and maintaining the worship of God.

A Church is "the body" of Christ, in its relation to him as "the head." It is "a spiritual temple," as being composed of spiritual or regenerate members, thus distinguished from all worldly organizations, It is "the pillar and ground of the truth," in its maintenance and support of the divine law, and its presentation, proclamation and propagation of the great and loving truths of the gospel.

Churches are divinely instituted to be the light of the world and the salt of the earth; they are ordained for the glory of God, in the proclamation of his gospel, and the establishment of his kingdom in the world. They exist for the edification of the saints and for the conversion of sinners, not for their own gratification or aggrandizement.

They should, therefore, be constantly striving to realize the great end of their existence, and fulfill the mission of their high calling, in earnest and devoted Christian work of every kind.

That church which is the most devoted and self-sacrficing for Christ, will certainly be the most successful and prosperous for itself.

Since a church is what its individual members are, in their religious life and influence, therefore each member should strive to become what he desires the church to be.

NOTE I.—A church is not to make laws, but only to administer and obey those which Christ has given in the New Testament. He is the only law-maker in Zion.

NOTE 2.—But in matters merely optional and discretionary, not involving fundamental principles in doctrine or order, the church is to exercise its liberty in judgment and direction, so long as it does not contravene Scriptural teaching, or infringe the rights of any.

NOTE 3.—The church is bound and under law to Christ; but, otherwise, it is independent of, and free from, the control and authority of all persons whatever, other than its own members.

NOTE 4.—The judgment and authority of the church is expressed in the vote of a majority of its members, after careful consideration. But the nearer that majority approaches to unanamity, the more satisfactory and emphatic are its authoritative decisions.

NOTE 5.—Committees for conference or reference may be selected, or councils called for advice in cases of difficulty. But they are advisory only, and in no instances authoritative. There is no higher and no other court of appeal in ecclesiastical affairs than the individual church.

ORDINANCES.

Baptism and the Lord's Supper are the only Scriptural ordinances of a Christian church.

BAPTISM.

1. *Baptism* is the immersion, or dipping, of a candidate in water, on a public profession of his faith in Christ, and on evidence of regeneration. And this baptism is to be performed by a suitable adminstrator, in the name of the Father, Son, and Holy Spirit.

No person can properly be received to membership in the church unless having thus been baptized; and, as baptism must precede an actual church membership, so it must precede all the privileges of church membership, including that of the Lord's Supper.

THE LORD'S SUPPER.

2. *The Lord's Supper* is a provision of bread and wine, partaken of by the members of the church; in which service they commemorate the sufferings and death of Christ for them, and profess their faith in him.

NOTE 1.—Both ordinances are ordinarily and properly administered by ordained and accredited ministers; but both would doubtless be equally valid if administered by private members, did occasion require and the church so direct.

NOTE 2.—While the privileges of the Lord's Supper can be claimed as a right only by the members of the particular church by which it is observed, yet it is customary, as an act of courtesy, to invite members of other Baptist churches, of like faith and order, who may be present at the administration, to remain and partake.

NOTE 3.—The communion and fellowship in the Supper is with Christ, "the head," and not with each other as "the members." "Do this in remembrance of *me*." All thought and sympathy in the service should be centred in him who is "the living bread," and not fixed on each other.*

***For a full discussion of controverted questions respecting Baptism and Communion see the "Baptist Short Method," by the author of this work.**

OFFICERS.

The officers of a church, according to New Testament teaching, are *pastors*, called also bishops, presbyters, elders and overseers; whose oversight, authority and duties are mainly in spiritual things; and *deacons*, whose official duties are chiefly an oversight of the temporal concerns of the church, and in general, as helpers of the pastor. The qualifications for both offices are set forth in the Epistles to Timothy and Titu

NOTE 1.—In the election of either a pastor or deacon, notice of such election should be given from the pulpit, for at least two Sundays preceding the time for the same. The election should be by ballot, and at least *three-quarters* of the votes cast should be necessary for the election of a pastor, and *two thirds* for the election of a deacon. And such elections should be preceded by prayer, and conducted without party influences.

NOTE 2.—Both pastor and deacons should be elected for unlimited time of service, and so long as there shall be mutual satisfaction. (Though deacons may sometimes be properly elected for a limited term.) Such a course tends less to depreciate and make servile the offices, and their duties, in the estimation of the people, and those who bear them, than limited periods of service.

NOTE 3.—The relation between the pastor and church may be dissolved at the option of either, by giving *three months* notice; or otherwise by mutual consent. Between the church and the deacons, the relation may be dissolved, at the option of either, without previous notice.

NOTE 4.—The church is to fix the amount of salary necessary to a generous support of the pastor, and hold itself obligated by every consideration of christian honor, for the prompt and regular payment of the same. To fail in this is as dishonorable to the church, as it is unjust and vexatious to the pastor.

NOTE 5.—The number of deacons is optional with the church. It is usually from *three* to *seven.* But election to the deaconship should never take place unless there are candidates whose fitness for the office is generally conceded; never merely for the sake of filling an office.

NOTE 6.—A church *clerk* is elected annually, at a business meeting, by a majority vote. It is an office of convenience, for keeping the minutes and preserving the records of the body. *Trustees* are also elected by the church, or, if the law makes this necessary, by a "society;" their duties are the care of the property and the management of finances.

NOTE 7.—The offices of trust, and service in a

church should be as widely distributed among the members as possible. This rule should seldom be transgressed. No one man should hold more than one office at the same time, unless it be a matter of positive necessity. If offices are honors, they should be widely dispensed. If they are burdens, they certainly should be. For the same man to hold two or three offices, is as unjust to him as it is to his brethren. To concentrate all official authority in the hands of a few, is virtually to constitute an oligarchy in the church ; a course as unwise practically, as it is opposed to the genius of the gospel. All experience and the widest observation, prove that such a course is the fruitful source of suspicion, discontent, partisanship, and strife in the household of faith. Relieve members of responsibility, and their interest declines. Give them too much power, and they may misuse it. Men positively unfit ought not to be put into office. But the best of men should not be tempted with too much office.

MEMBERSHIP.

Persons may become members of the church as follows:

1. By *Baptism;* the church, after having listened to their religious experience, and being satisfied with the same, and with their Christian deportment, votes to receive them to its fellowship on being baptized.

2. By *Letter;* such letter of dismission and recommendation being presented from another Baptist Church of the same faith and order, accompanied with satisfactory evidence of Christian character.

3. By *Experience;* they having been baptized, but being members of no church, or of another denomination; giving satisfactory evidence of Christian character, and of substantial agreement with the church in matters of faith and practice.

NOTE 1.—Persons can not be received to membership on the credit of letters from other denominations. Such letters will, however, be accepted as certificates of Christian character, and of church standing.

NOTE 2.—While the church does not require candidates to sign any creed, confession, or articles of faith, yet it does expect a substantial agreement in matters of faith and practice, on the part of its members, as essential both to the harmony and efficiency of the body.

NOTE 3.—Should any member object to the reception of a candidate, such reception should be deferred to consider the reasons for the objection. Objections judged groundless, or unreasonable, should not prevent the reception of a suitable candidate; yet no one should be received except by a unanimous or nearly unanimous vote.

NOTE 4.—It is customary for candidates, after their experience, or letters, have been presented, to retire while the church deliberates and acts upon their case.

NOTE 5.—Any member in good standing, shall be entitled, at any time, to a letter of dismission, in the usual form, with which to unite with another church of the same faith and order.

NOTE 6.—All letters shall be valid for *six months* only, during which time they must be used, if used at all. But if held longer, they may be renewed by the church, if satisfactory reasons are given for their non-use.

NOTE 7.—Each one receiving a letter is still a member of the church, and under its watch, care and discipline, until his letter is actually received by another church.

NOTE 8.—Letters cannot be given to members for the purpose of uniting with churches with which we are not in fellowship. But any member is entitled, at any time, to receive a certificate of standing, and Christian character.

NOTE 9.—No member can *withdraw* from the church, or have his name *dropped*, or at his own request be *excluded* from the fellowship of the body.

NOTE 10.—Nor can a member have a letter voted and forced upon him without his wish and consent. Such would be a virtual expulsion from the body. If worthy to receive a letter, he cannot be forced out of the church without his consent.

NOTE 11.—Members living remote from the church are expected to unite with some Baptist church near their residence; or give satisfactory reasons for not doing so. When they cannot so unite, they are expected to report themselves to the church at least once each year, and contribute to its support, till they cease to be members.

NOTE 12.—Letters of dismission may be revoked, at any time before being used, if, in the judgment of the church, there be sufficient reason for such action.

NOTE 13.—Church fellowship will be withdrawn from members who unite with other denominations; because, however excellent their character, or sincere their intentions, they have broken covenant with the church, and by such act have placed themselves beyond the limits of its fellowship.

NOTE 14.—Persons excluded from other churches cannot be received to membership, except after the most careful investigation of all the facts in the case, and not unless it be manifest that the exclusion was unjustifiable, and that the church excluding persistently refuses to do justice to the excluded member

NOTE 15.—A letter is usually asked for and addressed to a particular church. This is proper, but not necessary. It may be asked for, and given "to any church of the same faith and order." Or if directed to one, it may be presented to, and received by another.

NOTE 16.—It is expected that all pecuniary liability to the church will be canceled, and all personal difficulties in the church will be settled by a member, should such exist, before he asks for, or receives a letter of dismission.

NOTE 17.—Each member, without exception, is expected to fill his place in the church, in attendance on its appointments, as Providence may allow, and also to contribute of his means for the pecuniary support of the church, according to his ability. If in either of these respects he fails, and refuses. he becomes a covenant-breaker, and is subject to the discipline of the body.

DISCIPLINE.

In the adminstration of *corrective discipline*, for the settlement of difficulties, and the removal of offences, the church will be guided by the following rules and principles.

IN PRIVATE OFFENCES.

In *private offences*, or such as one member may commit against another member, occasioning a grievance which does not affect any other person or persons, the course prescribed by our Saviour, in Matthew, 18th chap., should be strictly followed.

1. *First Step.*—The member who considers himself injured must go to the offender, tell him his grief, and between themselves alone, if possible, adjust and settle the difficulty. "If thy brother shall trespass against thee, go and tell him his fault, between thee and him alone." This must be done, not to charge, upbraid, or condemn the offender, but to win him. "If he shall hear thee, thou hast gained thy brother."

2. *Second Step.*—If this shall fail, then the offended member must take one or two of the brethren with him, seek an interview with the offender, and, if possible, by their united wisdom and piety, remove the offence and harmonize the difficulty. "But if he will not hear thee, then take with thee one or two more, that in the mouth of

two or three witnesses every word may be established."

3. *Third Step.*—If this step should prove unavailing, then the offended member must tell the whole matter to the *church*, and leave it in their hands to be disposed of, as to them may seem wisest and best. "And if he shall neglect to hear them, tell it to the church; and if he neglect to hear the church, let him be unto thee as a heathen man, and a publican."

NOTE 1.—While this divine rule makes it obligatory on the offended member to go to the offender and seek a reconciliation, yet much more is it obligatory on any member who knows that a brother is grieved with him, to seek such an one, and try to remove the difficulty.

"If thou bring thy gift to the altar, and there rememberest that thy brother hath aught against thee, leave there thy gift before the altar, and go thy way; first be reconciled to thy brother, and then come and offer thy gift[1]."

NOTE 2.—The matter is not to be made public until these three steps have been fully taken, and have failed; and then to be made public only by telling the church, and no others.

NOTE 3.—When the case comes before the church, it must not be neglected, or dropped, but be judiciously pursued until the difficulty be adjusted, the offence removed, or else the offender be disfellowshipped, and put away.—1 Matt. v. 23.

In Public Offences.

Public offences are such as are supposed to be a reproach or an injury to the church as a body, or to the reputation of religion. They are not against any one person, more than another.

The more common causes of public offence are the following: False doctrine[1]; disregard of authority[2]; contention and strife[3]; immoral conduct[4]; disorderly walk[5]: covetous spirit[6]; arrogant conduct[7]; going to law[8].

The following is generally accepted as the proper course of treatment for public offences.

1. The first member who has knowledge of the offence, should, as in the case of private offences, seek the offender, ascertain the facts, and attempt to reconcile or remove the difficulty. Not till he has done this should he make it public, or bring it before the church.

2. But if no one will, or can, pursue this course of personal effort, or if such a course proves unsuccessful, then any member having knowledge of the facts should confer with the pastor and deacons, as to the best course to be pursued.

3. The pastor and deacons should, by the best

[1]Gal. i. 9.—2 John 12—[2]Matt. xviii. 17.—Thes. v. 14.— [3]Rom. xvii. 17.—[4]1 Cor. v. 11.—[5]2 Thes. iii. 6, 9.—[6]Eph. v. 5.—Cor. v. 11.—[7]3 John 9—.[8]1 Cor. vi. 6.

method they are capable of devising, labor to adjust the matter, without bringing it into the church, or otherwise making it public.

4. But if their efforts fail, or if the case be already public, and a reproach and scandal to religion, then they should bring it to the church, and direct the course of discipline as seems wisest.

5. The church, thus having the case before them, should either appoint a committee to visit the offender, or cite him before the body to answer the charge. He should be allowed to hear the evidence against him, know the witnesses, and be permitted to answer for himself.

6. If the accused disproves the charges, or if he confesses the wrong, makes suitable acknowledgement, and so far as possible reparation, with promise of amendment, in all ordinary cases, this should be deemed satisfactory, and the case be dismissed.

7. But if, after patient, deliberate, and prayerful labor, all efforts fail to reclaim the offender, then, however painful the necessity, the church must withdraw its fellowship from him, and put him away from them.

8. If the case be one of flagrant immorality, by which the reputation of the body is compromised, and the Christian name scandalized, the hand of fellowship should be withdrawn from the offender,

notwithstanding any confessions and promises of amendment.

The church's good name, and the honor of religion demands this testimony against evil. He may be subsequently restored if suitably penitent.

NOTE 1.—All discipline must be conducted in the spirit of Christian meekness and love, with a desire to remove offences, and win offenders. It must also be done under a deep sense of responsibility to maintain the honor of Christ's name, the purity of his church, and integrity of his truth.

NOTE 2.—If any member shall attempt to bring a private grievance before the church, or otherwise make it public, before he has pursued the course prescribed in Matthew, xviii. chapter, he becomes himself an offender, and subject to the discipline of the body.

NOTE 3.—When private difficulties exist among members, which they cannot, or will not settle, the church should consider them as public offences, and as such dispose of them, rather than suffer the perpetual injury which they inflict.

NOTE 4.—When a member refers any private difficulty to the church, which he has been unable to settle, he must submit it wholly to the disposition of the body, and abide by their decision. If he attempts to revive and prosecute it beyond the decision of the church, he becomes an offender, and subject to discipline.

NOTE 5.—Any member tried by the church has the right to receive copies of all charges against him, the names of his accusers and witnessess, both of whom he shall have the privilege of meeting face to face, hearing their statements, bringing witnesses on his side, and answering for himself before the body.

NOTE 6.—Every member, on trial, or excluded, shall have furnished, at his request, authentic copies of all prcoeedings had by the church in his a e.

NOTE 7.—No member under discipline can have the right to bring any person, not a member, before the church as his advocate, except by consent of the body.

NOTE 8.—In every case of exclusion, the charges against the member, and the reasons for his exclusion, should be accurately entered on the records of the church.

NOTE 9.—If at any time it shall become apparent, or seem probable to the church, that it has for any reason dealt unjustly with a member, or excluded him without sufficient cause, it should at once, and without request, by concession and restoration, so far as possible repair the injury it has done.

NOTE 10.—The church should hold itself bound to restore to its fellowship an excluded member whenever he gives satisfactory evidence of repentance and reformation consistent with godliness.

NOTE 11.—The church will exercise its legitimate authority, and vindicate its honor and rectitude in the adminstration of discipline, even though the member should regard such discipline as unjust or oppressive.

NOTE 12.—Nothing can be considered a just and reasonable cause for discipline except what is forbidden by the letter or the spirit of Scripture. And nothing can be considered a sufficient cause for disfellowship and exclusion, except what is clearly contrary to Scripture, and what would have prevented the reception of the person into the church, had it been known to exist at the time of his reception.*

CHURCH BUSINESS.

The business meetings of the church should be conducted as much as possible in the spirit of devotion, and under a sense of the propriety and sanctity which attaches to the kingdom of God.

*For a comprehensive view of Church order and discipline, see that subject in "The Baptist Church Directory."

Order of Business.

1. The meetings to be opened with reading the Scriptures, singing, and prayer.

2. The reading, correction, and approval of the minutes of the preceding meeting.

3. Unfinished business, or such as the minutes present, including reports of committee taken in order.

4. New business will next be taken up. Any member may call up new business. But important matters should not be presented, except on previous consultation with the pastor and deacons.

NOTE 1.— The pastor is, by virtue of his office, moderator of all church business meetings. If he be not present, or do not wish to serve, any one may be elected to take the place.

NOTE 2.—All business meetings should be announced from the pulpit one sabbath at least, before they are held.

NOTE 3.—Special meetings for business may be called at any time, by consent of the pastor and deacons.

NOTE 4.—Though a majority usually decides questions, yet in all matters of special importance, a unaminous, or nearly unaminous, vote should be secured.

NOTE 5.—Members may be received, and letters of dismission granted, either at the business church meeting, the covenant meeting, or the regular weekly prayer meeting, the church so directing.

NOTE 6.—Candidates for admission to membership will be expected to retire from the meeting when action is taken on their reception.

NOTE 7.—No persons, except members, will be expected to be present during the transaction of church business. If present, they may be asked to retire.

NOTE 8.—Although the church should endeavor to do nothing which its members will be ashamed or afraid to have known by others, yet every member is bound, by the honor of a Christian, not to publish abroad, nor disclose to those without, the private affairs and business transactions of the body.

RULES OF ORDER.

The following constitute the generally accepted rules of order for church, and other business proceedings.

Motions.

1. All business shall be presented by a *motion*, made by one member, and seconded by another, and presented in writing by the mover, if so required.

2. No discussion can properly be had until the motion is made, seconded, and stated by the chairman.

3. A motion cannot be withdrawn after it has been discussed, except by the unanimous consent of the body.

4. A motion having been discussed, must be put to vote, unless withdrawn, laid on the table, referred, or postponed.

5. A motion lost should not be recorded, except so ordered by the body at the time.

6. A motion lost cannot be renewed at the same meeting, except by unanimous consent.

7. A motion should contain but one distinct proposition. If it contains more, it must be divided at the request of any member, and the propositions acted on separately.

8. Only one question can properly be before the meeting at the same time. No second motion can be allowed to interrupt one already under debate, except a motion to *amend*, to *substitute*, to *commit*, to *postpone*, to *lay on the table*, for *the previous question*, or to *adjourn*.

9. These subsidiary motions just named, cannot be interrupted by any other motion ; nor can any other motion be applied to them, except that to *amend*, which may be done by specifying some *time*, *place*, or *purpose*.

10. Nor can these motions interrupt or supersede each other; only that a motion to *adjourn* is always in order, except while a member has the floor, or a question is being taken.

Amendments.

1. Amendments may be made to resolutions in three ways: By *omitting*, by *adding*, or by *substituting* words or sentences.

2. An amendment to an amendment may be made, but is seldom necessary, and should be avoided.

3. No amendment should be made which essentially changes the meaning or design of the original resolution.

4. But a *substitute* may be offered, which may change entirely the meaning of the resolution under debate.

5. The amendment must first be discussed and acted on, and then the original resolution as amended.

Speaking.

1. Any member desiring to speak on a question, should rise in his place, and address the moderator, confine his remarks to the question, and avoid all unkind and disrespectful language.

2. A speaker using improper language, introducing improper subjects, or otherwise out of

order, should be called to order by the chairman, or any member, and must either conform to the regulations of the body, or take his seat.

3. A member, while speaking, can allow others to ask questions, or make explanations; but if he yields the floor to another, he cannot claim it again as his right.

4. If two members rise to speak at the same time, preference is usually given to the one farthest from the chair, or to the one opposing the question under discussion.

5. The fact that a person has several times arisen, and attempted to get the floor, gives him no claim or right to be heard. Nor does a call for the question deprive a member of his right to speak.

Voting.

1. A question is put to vote by the chairman, having first distinctly re-stated it, that all may vote intelligently. First, the *affirmative*, then the *negative* is called; each so deliberately as to give all an opportunity of voting. He then distinctly announces whether the motion is *carried*, or *lost*.

2. Voting is usually done by "aye" and "no," or by raising the hand. In a doubtful case, by standing, and being counted. On certain questions, by ballot.

3. If the vote, as announced by the chairman, is doubted, it is called again, usually by standing to be counted.

4. All members should vote, unless for reasons excused ; or unless under discipline, in which case they should take no part in the business.

5. The moderator does not usually vote, except the question be taken by ballot ; but when the meeting is equally divided, he usually gives the casting vote.

6. When the vote is to to be taken by ballot, the chairman appoints *tellers*, to distribute, collect, and count the ballots.

Committees.

1. Committees are nominated by the chairman, if so directed by the body, or by any member ; and the nomination is confirmed by a vote of the body. More commonly the body directs that all committees shall be *appointed* by the chairman, in which case no vote is needed to confirm.

2. Any matter of business, or subject under debate, may be *referred* to a committee, with or without instructions. The committee make their *report*, which is the result of their deliberations. The body then takes action on the report, and on any recommendations it may contain.

3. The report of a committee is *received* by a vote, which acknowledges their services, and takes

the report before the body for its action. Afterwards, any distinct *recommendation* contained in the report is acted on, and may be adopted or rejected.

4. Frequently, however, when the recommendations of the committee are of trifling moment, or likely to be generally acceptable, the report is *received* and *adopted* by the same vote.

5. A report may be *recommitted* to the committee, with or without instructions; or that committee discharged, and the matter referred to a new one, for further consideration, so as to present it in a form more likely to meet the general concurrence of the body.

6. A committee may be appointed *with power*, for a specific purpose. This gives them power to dispose conclusively of the matter, without further reference, or report to the body.

7. The first named in the appointment of a committee, is by courtesy considered the chairman. But the committee has the right to name its own chairman.

8. The member who moves the appointment of a committee is usually, though not necessarily, named its chairman.

9. The committees of arrangement, or for other protracted service, *report progress* from time to time, and are continued until their final report, or until their appointment expires by limitation.

10. A committee is *discharged* by a vote, when its business is done, and its report accepted. But usually, in routine business, a committee is considered discharged by the acceptance of its report.

Standing Committee.

A committee appointed to act for a given period or during the recess of the body, is called a *standing committee.* It has charge of a given department of business assigned by the body, and acts either with power, under instruction, or at discretion, as may be ordered. A standing committee is substantially a minor board, and has its own chairman, secretary, records, and times of meeting.

Appeal.

The moderator announces all votes, and decides all questions as to rules of proceeding, and order of debate. But any member who is dissatisfied with his decisions, may *appeal* from them to the body. The moderator then puts the question, "*Shall the decision of the chair be sustained?*" The vote of the body, whether negative or affirmative, is final. The right of appeal is undeniable, but should not be resorted to on trivial occasions.

Previous Question.

Debate may be cut short, by a vote to take the *previous question*. This means that the original, or main question under discussion, be immediately voted on, regardless of amendments and secondary questions, and without further debate.

1. If the motion for the previous question be *carried*, then the main question must be immediately taken, without further debate.

2. If the motion for the previous question be *lost*, the debate proceeds, as though no such motion had been made.

3. If the motion for the previous question be *lost*, it cannot be renewed with reference to the same question, during that session.

To Lay on the Table.

Immediate and decisive action on any question under discussion may be deferred, by a vote to *lay on the table* the resolution pending. This disposes of the whole subject for the present, and ordinarily is in effect a final dismissal of it. But any member has the right subsequently to call it up; and the body will decide by vote whether, or not, it shall be taken from the table.

1. Sometimes, however, a resolution is laid on the table for the present, or until a specified time to give place to other business.

2. A motion to lay on the table must apply to a resolution, or other papers. An abstract subject cannot be disposed of in this way.

Postponement.

A simple *postponement* is for a specified time or purpose, the business to be resumed when the time or purpose is reached. But a question *indefinitely postponed* is considered as finally dismissed.

Not Debatable.

Certain motions, by established usage, are *not debatable*, but when once before the body, must be taken without discussion.

These are: The *previous question*, for *indefinite postponement*, to *commit*, to *lay on the table*, to *adjourn*.

But when these motions are modified by some condition of *time*, *place*, or *purpose*, they become debatable, and subject to the rules of other motions.

A body is, however, competent, by a vote, to allow debate on all motions.

To Reconsider.

A motion to *reconsider* a motion previously passed, must be made by one who voted *for* the motion when it passed.

If the body votes to reconsider, then the motion or resolution, being reconsidered, stands before them as previous to its passage, and may be discussed, adopted or rejected.

A vote to reconsider should be taken at the same session at which the vote reconsidered was passed, and when there are as many members present.

Be Discussed.

If, when a question is introduced, any member objects to its discussion, as foreign, profitless, or contentious, the moderator should at once put the question, "*Shall this motion be discussed?*" If this question be decided in the negative, the subject must be dismissed.

Order of the Day.

The body may decide to take up some definite business at a specified time. That business thereby becomes the *order of the day*, for that hour. When the time mentioned arrives, the chairman calls the business, or any member may demand it, with or without a vote; and all pending questions are postponed in consequence.

Point of Order.

Any member who believes that a speaker is out of order, or that discussion is proceeding improperly, may at any time *rise to a point of order*. He must distinctly state his question or objection, which the moderator will decide.

Privileges.

Questions relating to the *rights* and *privileges* of members, are of primary importance, and, until disposed of, take precedence of all other business, and supersede all other motions, except that of adjournment.

Rule Suspended.

A rule of order may be *suspended* by a vote of the body, to allow the transaction of business necessary, but which could not otherwise be done without a violation of such rule.

Filling Blanks.

Where different numbers are suggested for filling blanks, the *highest number*, *greatest distance*, and *longest time* are usually voted on first.

Adjournment.

1. A simple motion *to adjourn* is always in order, except while a member is speaking, or when taking a vote. It takes precedence of all other motions, and is not debatable.

2. In some deliberative bodies, a motion to adjourn is in order while a speaker has the floor, or a vote is being taken, the business to stand, on reassembling, precisely as when adjournment took place.

3. A body may adjourn to a specified time; but if no time be mentioned, the fixed, or usual time of meeting is understood. If there be no fixed, or usual time of meeting, then an adjournment without date, is equivalent to a dissolution.

NOTE.—While it may not be best to abide too rigidly by parliamentary rules in church meetings, yet it is still worse to drift into a loose, unbusiness-like way, which wastes time, accomplishes little, and does wrongly much that is done.

STANDING RESOLUTIONS.

There are certain moral and social questions which often occasion perplexity, with respect to which each church should have settled convictions, and hold a well-defined attitude.

It is not wise to put definitions and restrictions touching intemperance, card-playing, dancing, theater-going, and the like, into church covenants, or articles of faith. A better way is to vote standing resolutions, to be placed on the records to guide the action of the church.

Something like the following, to be varied at the option of the body, would serve as a declaration of its position:

1. *Resolved*, That this Church will expect each member to contribute statedly for its support, according to his ability, as God hath prospered him.

2. *Resolved*, That this Church will entertain and contribute statedly to the leading objects of Christian benevolence approved of, and supported by our denomination.

3. *Resolved*, That the religious education of the young, and Bible study as represented in Sunday-School work, commend themselves to our confidence, and we will, to the extent of our ability, give them our sympathy and our aid, by both our personal co-operation and our contributions.

4. *Resolved*, That in our opinion, the use of intoxicating drinks as a beverage, and, also, the manufacture and the sale of the same, for such a use, are contrary to Christian morality, injurious to personal piety, and a hindrance to Gospel truth ; and that persons so using, making, or selling, are thereby disqualified for membership in this Church.

5. *Resolved*, That we emphatically condemn the practice of church members attending theatres and other similar places of popular amusement, as inconsistant with a Christian profession, detrimental to personal piety, and pernicious in the influence of its example on others.

6. *Resolved*, That the members of this Church are earnestly requested not to provide for, take part in, or by any means encourage dancing, or card-playing ; but in all consistant ways to discountenance the same, as harmful to godliness in their associations and tendencies, and an offence to brethren whom we should not willingly grieve.

FORMS AND BLANKS.

Minutes of a Church Meeting.

NEW YORK, Oct. —, 18—.

THE Church held its regular meeting for business this evening, at — o'clock

The Pastor: Moderator.

After singing, and reading the Scriptures, prayer was offered by ——.

Minutes of the last meeting were read and approved.

[Then follows an accurate record of all the business done,]

The meeting adjourned.

————, Clerk.

Call for an Ordaining Council.

NEW YORK, Oct. —, 18--.

The —— Church of ——

To the —— Church of ——

DEAR BRETHREN:

You are requested to send your pastor and two delegates, to meet in council with us, Nov. —, at — o'clock A. M., to consider the propriety of publicly setting apart to the work of the Gospel ministry, our brother —— ——.

The Council will meet in ——.

The following churches are invited—— .

By order of the Church,

————Clerk.

Call for a Recognizing Council.

NEW YORK, Oct. —, 18—.

To the ——— Church of ———

DEAR BRETHREN:

In behalf of a company of believers in Christ, you are requested to send your pastor and two delegates, to meet in council at———, Nov. —, at — o'clock P.M., to consider the propriety of recognizing said company of believers as a regular and independent Church.

The Council will meet in ———.

The following churches are invited———.

Affectionately yours,

——————— Com. or Clerk.

NOTE.—By some, it is earnestly contended, that a council to recognize a church, should be called to render its advice *before* the church is constituted, and not afterwards. Advice asked, or given after the act is consummated, seems a meaningless service.

Call for an Advisory Council.

NEW YORK, Oct. —, 18 —.

The ——— Church of ———

To the ———Church of ———

DEAR BRETHREN:

You are requested to send your pastor and two delegates, to meet in council, Nov. —, at — o'clock P. M., to advise concerning certain difficulties existing among us, which disturb our peace, and threaten the most serious consequences to the welfare of the Church.

The Council will be held in———.

The following churches are invited————.

By order of the Church,

——— ———, Clerk.

Letter of Dismission.

The Church of ———

To the ——— Church of ———

DEAR BRETHREN:

This is to certify that ——— is a member of this Church in good and regular standing, and, at — own request, is hereby dismissed from us, to unite with you. When — shall have so united, — connection with us will cease. May the blessing of God rest on ———, and on you.

Done by order of the Church, New York, Oct. —, 18—. ——————— Clerk.

This letter is valid for six months from date.

NOTE.—It is customary for a letter to be asked for and given, to unite with a particular Church, to be named in the letter. But it may be asked for, and given to "any Church of the same faith and order." If given to a specified Church, it may be used for any other similar Church, if thought necessary.

Letter of Commendation.

This certifies that ——— ——— is a member in good and regular standing, of the ——— Church of ———; and as such, I most cordially commend — to the confidence, sympathy, and fellowship of sister churches, wherever Providence may direct — course. ——— ———, Pastor.

NOTE.—Such a letter is given to members during a temporary absence from home, and as an introduction among strangers.

www.ingramcontent.com/pod-product-compliance
Lightning Source LLC
Chambersburg PA
CBHW021521090426
42739CB00007B/711

* 9 7 8 3 3 3 7 0 4 3 2 1 6 *